CORNELIUS LEARNS

About

ILLUSTRATED BY
MARIAM KEINA

WRITTEN BY
CHARLOTTE DANE

CONFIRMATION BIAS

CORNELIUS LEARNS ABOUT CONFIRMATION BIAS

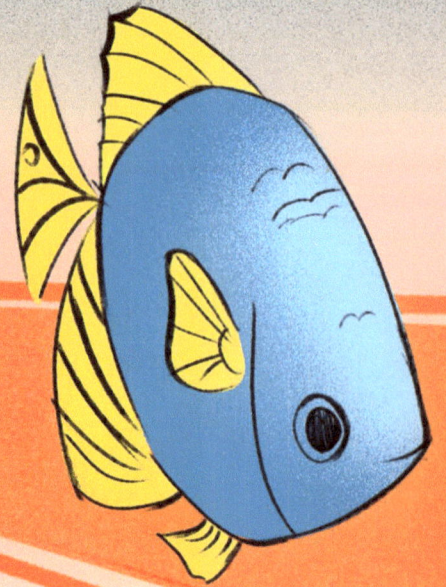

Sometimes when we believe something,
we only see what we want to see.

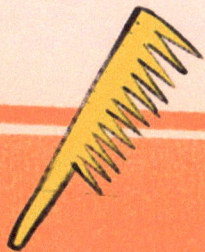

This is a very dangerous habit called confirmation bias, and it's when we are unable to see what other people might believe. But it's a habit that Cornelius was amazing at conquering.

Cornelius never just saw what he wanted to see. He knew his belief was only one of many, so he made sure to find as many as possible! Only then could he make a great decision.

But Cornelius wasn't always so open-minded. In fact, he used to drop into his belief with no way of getting out. It was like he got sucked into it.

STYLER Z BIKE

HEALTHIER

WORSE DESIGN

SLOWER

OLDER TECH

CHEAPER

ECO FRIENDLY

For example, one time Cornelius decided that the Styler Z bike was the best bike available. He saw it in the store window and couldn't stop staring!

B TYPE COMMUTER BIKE

RACER INFINITI

IDEAL FOR LONG DISTANCES

1 PROFESSIONAL USE

HIGHER QUALITY

MORE COMFORTABLE

FASTER

EXPENSIVE

FUEL ENGINE

But before buying it, he made sure to collect more information about other models, and he discovered that the Racer Infiniti was actually the best bike available. Good thing he didn't believe his first instinct!

For example, one time at summer camp, Cornelius believed that all ponies are just baby horses. (They aren't!)

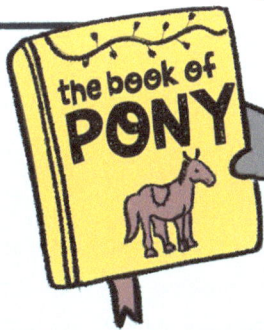

When one of the camp counselors showed him the dictionary, Cornelius said that the dictionary was wrong!

Another time, Cornelius believed that chocolate was one of the healthiest foods for a kitty like him. (It's not!)

DIET
-BOOK-

He even asked his vet, and when the vet told Cornelius to avoid chocolate, he thought that the vet's information must be outdated.

Finally, last summer, he believed that there were sharks at the beach near his home. (There weren't!)

Cornelius asked a life guard, and after the life guard said there weren't any sharks, Cornelius just figured that his binoculars weren't good enough.

Why did Cornelius sometimes remain stuck inside his own beliefs, even when there was evidence against them?

It was because he had already made the decision that his belief was correct. When you decide that you are correct, everything else is wrong.

Cornelius met his friend Charlotte one day for a stroll, and they came upon a nice big oak tree.

Charlotte wanted to have a climb, but Cornelius believed that climbing trees was bad for your eyes. Charlotte was an eye doctor and told him it wasn't true, but Cornelius didn't believe her!

Charlotte saw what was happening. She said, "Cornelius, I think you might be doing things backwards. You are starting with a belief and then finding evidence for it."

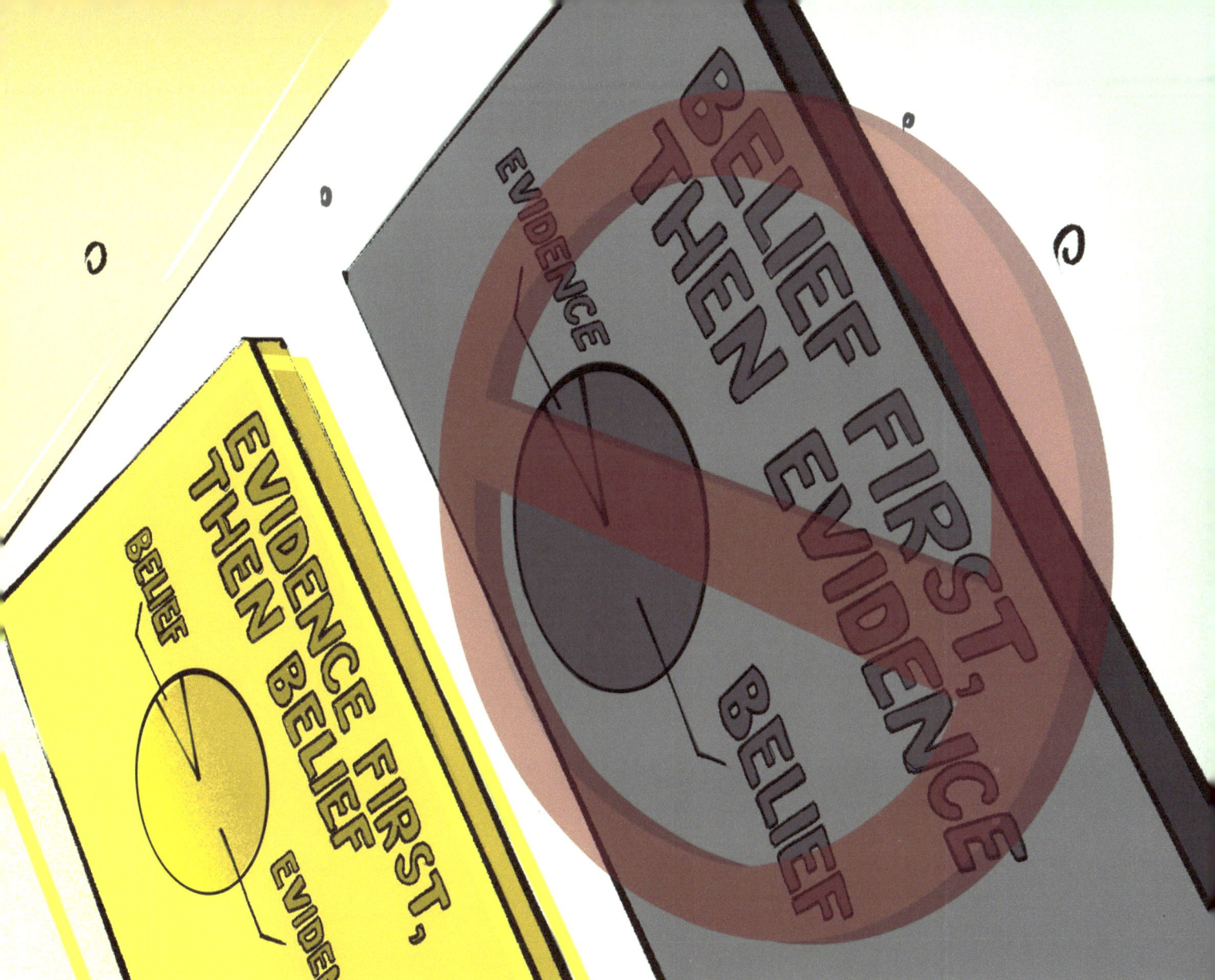

EVIDENCE FIRST, THEN BELIEF

BELIEF

EVIDENCE

BELIEF FIRST, THEN EVIDENCE

EVIDENCE

BELIEF

"This will lead to something called confirmation bias, where nothing can change your belief. We should actually do the opposite, which is to first see all the evidence, and only then have a belief, opinion, or judgment."

"Let me teach you something that will help you be more open-minded, even if you already have a belief. It's called the Scout Rule."

"A scout is someone who explores and collects information from all the perspectives they can, and they do this all without forming a belief. The scout just wants to know what the big picture looks like."

Charlotte said, "The easiest way to be a scout is to ask yourself 'What if I'm wrong?' because then you can start to think differently. Because you let yourself think of other possibilities!"

"If you start at one end, and then use the opposite perspective, then there's lots of room to think and find what the most balanced belief is!"

Charlotte said, "This is the first step to avoiding confirmation bias and being open-minded."

"You see, when you show two people the same thing, they can see completely different things. It's important for you to be able to do this too."

Charlotte said, "Even the smartest people might forget that their belief or opinion isn't reality! The Scout Rule is just a reminder that you might not always be correct or see things clearly."

Cornelius asked, "Even Albert Einstein?" Charlotte replied, "Yes, even him! Everyone needs to double check from time to time."

Cornelius thought back to his belief that chocolate was the healthiest food he could eat.

He used the Scout Rule and asked himself "What if he was wrong?" What if the vet was correct? What is his belief was a misinterpretation? What if he actually misunderstood what he heard? He started to think about the issue completely differently! He could suddenly see evidence that he previously ignored. He realized that he was quite close-minded before, and could now start to see how smart other perspectives could be.

Sometimes, despite our best efforts, we can only see a cloudy version of reality. But the Scout Rule is like having an amazing radar system that lets you see through the clouds to the real landscape.

Everyone sees the world as they want, not as it is.
The only thing we can do is try, try, try!

Cornelius thought back to his belief that sharks were at the beach.

What if he was wrong? What if sharks were not at the beach? What if sharks would never swim that far? What if his belief was a mixup? What if they were actually dolphins? Then the life guard was correct. Then it was safe. Then he could swim for hours. It was that simple!

In this humorous book, Cornelius the Cat learns a valuable lesson about confirmation bias, and how to see the beliefs and perspectives of others. Confirmation bias can be a real issue in your growing child and how they think and learn! Come learn along with Cornelius and see exactly how to conquer this problem and ensure academic, social, and emotional growth.

The "I think..." series is a children's book series aimed at arming children with essential thinking skills and mental models. You can never start too early to ensure that your child knows how to make great decisions. To learn more, go to BigBarnPress.com

www.ingramcontent.com/pod-product-compliance
Lightning Source LLC
Chambersburg PA
CBHW042023090426

42811CB00016B/1715